Published 2016 by Geddes & Grosset,
an imprint of The Gresham Publishing Company Ltd,
Academy Park, Building 4000, Gower Street,
Glasgow, G51 1PR, Scotland.

Reprinted 2018

Copyright © 1998 The Gresham Publishing Company Ltd.

Illustrations by Sue King.

All rights reserved. No part of this publication may be reproduced, stored in a retrieval system or transmitted in any form or by any means, electronic, mechanical, photocopying, recording or otherwise, without the prior permission of the copyright holder.

Conditions of Sale:
This book is sold with the condition that it will not, by way of trade or otherwise, be resold, hired out, lent, or otherwise distributed or circulated in any form or style of binding or cover other than that in which it is published and without the same conditions being imposed on the subsequent purchaser.

ISBN 978-1-910965-43-6

Printed and bound in Malaysia.

Smile!

by
Judy Hamilton

When you need a little sunshine on a dreary day,
When you want to feel better, and chase the gloom away,

Stretch your lips and show your teeth – give a great big grin.

SMILE! Send the grumps away, let happiness come in!

SMILE to see the sunshine on a summer's day.

SMILE to see soft green grass and lots of space to play!

SMILE to say "Thank you, that was very kind!"

SMILE to help when someone is sad.
A SMILE says "Never mind!"

When visitors come calling,
SMILE and say "Hello!"

Then SMILE and wave, say "See you soon!" when it's time for them to go.

SMILE for the camera!
Say "sausages!" or "cheese!"

SMILE when you ask for something – and remember to say "Please"!

SMILE when you are all dressed up – don't you look grand!

SMILE to say "I like you!
Will you be my friend?"

SMILE when you are busy!
A smile makes it more fun!

SMILE when you have finished and the job's all done!

SMILE when it's better –
no more tears!

SMILE to show that you've done well.
SMILE and give three cheers!

When a brother or sister comes
back home.
At the end of a long school day,

A SMILE says "I missed you when you were away!"

SMILE to say, "I'm glad you're here, I like to be with you!"

A great big SMILE can say,
"I love you!"

Tears happen sometimes when things go wrong.
But a cross face is hard work – you can't be cross for long!

Frowns look funny, crumpled
 up and tight,
But a smile fits your face
 and makes it look just right.

A SMILE is magic!
 See what it can do!
SMILE at people – and sure enough

They will SMILE right back at you!